A FEEL FOR GOD

*How to Better
Understand the Lord*

Michael J Spyker

AgapeDeum

Published in Adelaide, Australia by AgapeDeum
Contact: agapedeum.com

ISBN	paperback	9780645772043
	ebook	9780645772050

Copyright © Michael J Spyker 2023

All right reserved. Other than for the purpose and subject to the conditions prescribed under the *Copyright Act*, no part of this publication may be reproduced, stored in a retrieval system, or transmitted in any form or by any means, electronic, mechanical, photocopying, recording and otherwise, without prior permission of the publisher.

Publication assistance by Immortalise

Cover design: Ben Morton

Original artwork: Starry Night by Vincent Van Gogh, Public Domain.

CONTENT

Chapter 1	A Feel for God	1
Chapter 2	The One Who Is	6
Chapter 3	Love that IS	10
Chapter 4	A Mundane God	13
Chapter 5	Good Enough	16
Chapter 6	Love and Logic	20
Chapter 7	Rhyme nor Reason	25
Chapter 8	Invitation or Submission	29
Chapter 9	Enthused or Excited	33
Chapter 10	Child or Champion	37
Chapter 11	Faith and Fragmentation	42
Chapter 12	Rest or Restive	46
Chapter 13	Conscience and Compassion	50
Chapter 14	Angry or Aggrieved	54
Chapter 15	Agapino	58

1

A Feel for God

Much of how God is presented is derived from the religious knowledge industry: the Jewish and Christian traditions and the many books written over millennia. What God is like and the nature of humanity has been continually interpreted in accordance with the wisdom and culture of the times. In these modern days, I have been a keen participant in this search for understanding. It has shaped me and given insights I treasure. Is it then the theologically educated who best know what God is about? I wouldn't think so.

Jesus, for one, had a low regard for how the Jewish religious leaders of his day were guiding the common person. Often he was at loggerheads with the religious authorities and at a given moment accused them of having the Devil as their father (John 8: 44). His own conversations with people were simple and relevant to daily life. Frequently, they were also confusing. What Jesus said then remains open to discussion also today whereby a little knowledge may come in handy. Often though it needs a feel for God, sensed within the soul, to have the Lord best understood.

A transcendent presence in our world has been detected by people from the beginning of human existence. In need of finding a measure of security under this unknown greater reality modes of worship and story-telling evolved to appease the gods and encourage their engagement in human pursuits. Holy places and idols became part of this effort. The figure of an idol could represent nature, like a golden calf, or gods that had a human appearance like in ancient Greece and Rome. Hindu gods may display a mix of human and animal in their conceptualisation while to Buddhism the idea of god is totally foreign. Accordingly, it is suggested that Buddhism is more a philosophy than a true religion. Whatever the case, it does engage the transcendental realm.

The Israelites understood that One God, who should never be depicted, is what interacting with the divine realm is about. This God is so magnificent and beyond human reality that it is blasphemy to verbalise the name Yahweh. Not so secondary names like Elohim. God is holy and all-knowing, creator of the universe. God could be fierce as well as benevolent. The history of Israel as presented in the Old Testament shows how the Jews interpreted the presence of this majesty dwelling above and amongst them.

The arrival of Jesus of Nazareth walking through Israel declaring himself the Son of God suggested a shift in the understanding of God that the religious leaders of the Jews could not accept. One can hardly blame them. People were encouraged by Jesus to call the magnificent, holy God their heavenly Father. The divine majesty thought to be dwelling far away and approachable in fear and trembling was suggested to be fully relational and imminently present. The significance of this was only grasped over time with the development of Christianity.

Jesus selected the idea of a heavenly Father as culturally best in describing what God is really like. Like a good father, who is capable and who cares. God is without gender and can carry the name Mother equally so. Medieval mystic Lady Julian of Norwich referred to Jesus our Mother, which considering that all of creation has been birthed in Christ, makes good sense. The mystery of God is wonderful.

Cognitive understanding alone will not do justice to this mystery. It must be penetrated by intuition also – by having a feel for God. But how might someone develop such a feel? Prayer and its many modes of expression is a way and a necessary one. Personally, I much enjoy reflective prayer. There is a further way, readily available, that allows for a feel for God. It originates from the understanding that people exist as an image of God. Their humanity can express what God is like. Everyone is able to do so, with Christians having that reality quickened within them by the Holy Spirit.

It is quite simple, really. Everything that is good within a person represents the nature of God. Whatever is negative and destructive comes from sinful influences and is anti-God. A feel for God is developed by focusing on the good within me for it embodies what God is like. I take that feel into all I am faced with and seek to live accordingly. I will judge world affairs in light of this understanding. I am aware that developing the right feel for God requires humility and kindness. It will prevent the ego from manipulating the senses.

Always a feel for God is coloured by the ideas held about God. How to incorporate an understanding of the nature of divine reality into everyday life is the topic to be discussed. *A Feel for God* is the third book in a series and is preceded by *Walking with God* and *Being with God*. Insights from each may overlap at times but will complement each other. I have always found being introduced to different aspects of an idea helpful.

This series of three short books written in easy language and clear concepts aims to assist in finding intimacy with the Lord whatever the circumstances. Having the right feel for God has helped me in understanding the Lord much better.

2

The One Who IS

What's in a name? It is an interesting question. A name can mean a lot, or little. I have a friend John and know him well. John means a lot to me, not because of his name but for who he is. My friend K.K. also has a friend called John, but I have never met him. This John means little to me. So, indeed, what's in a name? Nothing much in the name itself but everything that the bearer stands for. Names are identifiers that allow for social recognitions. A boat is named a boat for what it is capable of. The Blue Dolphin is a particular boat with a unique history that sets it apart. Names are helpful. But why this philosophical introduction when discussing a feel for God?

Well, the Jewish God has no name. The word god is a classification that signifies transcendence and as such not a name. The gods must be named and are. Hinduism has thousands of them each with their particular characteristics. A god with a name and a given magic can be easily identified with. Like the god of fertility or war. The One God of Israel and Christianity is not thus named for how do you label the Creator of the universe who represents not a particular but 'everything' and beyond?

When Moses met with the God of Israel at the burning bush and was given instructions to liberate God's people out of Egypt, he asked who he should tell them had sent him. The answer was not a name but a reference to Ultimate Being. Tell them 'I AM' sent you (Ex. 3:14). God is the great 'I AM'. I rather like that. It feels better than the word 'God', definitely more dynamic. The Jewish idea of not speaking out the true name of God, even though God doesn't have one, may not be such a bad idea. It recognises that the One God exceeds the boundaries of creation. Instead the Israelites used names that represented attributes of God like, El Shaddai, God the Almighty.

Jesus introduced God as a Father in heaven. The word 'father' is not a name but a category of being. The idea of the Father reveals what God essentially is about. But it has its downsides in being gender specific. The feel of the word can stir up adverse emotions. I had a friend who found difficulty in relating to God due to his childhood experiences. When I told him that God is as much mother as father he became excited. 'So God is like my mother', he said, much relieved. 'Now that's a God can relate to.' His father had mistreated him.

In my writing I avoid gender in reference to God and use the word Lord intermittingly. With Jesus there is no such problem, of course. He is the human side of God and spiritually readily identified with. I find it interesting that in general church preaching tends to focus more on God than on Jesus. Perhaps because an opaque, distant God is easier talked about than the immediacy of the personhood of Christ. Recently, I was twice confronted with Christians referring to God as 'the universe.' Comments like, 'I leave it to the universe.' The One God, who is beyond naming, becomes identified not as ultimate being but by a created realtiy. It may seem harmless, just a throw-away line (used in modern theology), but it is not and must be avoided.

How then will I get a feel for the unnamed God, whose majesty is well beyond me? Being born in the image of God means there is a correlation between what God is like and my personhood. A feel for the great I AM comes about by being open to it in spirit. Reaching out for that 'feel', when seriously done, will find a noticeable response within the soul. Seek it, believe in it, and in doing so the presence of God becomes real. Be still and know that I AM. It is a mystery but it works. Once discerned, the divine presence must be kept fresh by a daily reaching out.

As with everything involving God, faith and confidence are essential. Doubts are normal but must be waylaid. The feel of the embracing love of God is nurtured by understanding, and living in accordance with, the nature of God. It is what the remainder our discussion will mostly address.

3

Love that IS

God *is* Love. It is the basis of my theological understanding spurred on by a vision I once had of divine love, when the Lord momentarily lifted the veil somewhat regarding the Trinity. That experience showed me that God is not so much loving, but exists as a love that IS. Only the Godhead encapsulates that reality. Like I cannot but be Michael Spyker in all I express. What I am, is what I am without fail. Thus God IS love inescapably. God cannot be or act otherwise.

When Jesus asked Julian of Norwich whether she was well satisfied with what he had achieved for her on the cross, she was told that if he would have had to die thus for every person individually, he would have done so. I wouldn't even want to contemplate such as situation, but it highlights the unlimited love of God for creation. How beyond imagination that love is. Had it been required, that love simply would have had Jesus die again and again out of necessity, driven by its very nature and unlimited capacity.

I have some idea what love is about and once deeply fell in love, and still am in love, with my wife. Falling in love is not something God can do for what you are in its fullness cannot be added to. My experiences of love are incomplete and, because of sin, only a reflection of the divine nature. Once that limitation is taken away in heaven, I will exist solely in the unrestricted love of God. I have no idea what that will be like but it must be fabulous.

God does not expect me to comprehend the divine love. Simply, it is not possible. I have been helped by the vision I had, which I'm deeply grateful for. But the true magnitude of God's unimaginable love towards me, and everyone, I accept by faith. Everything about God and the divine plan becomes real within a person by faith. Faith is the conviction of things not seen. This can be a stumbling block or a blessing. I like worshiping a God of love who is far too big and powerful for me to understand and completely transcends our universe. I am invited to believe in this God for divine reality to become a blessing to me. A reality I may willingly engage with and that transforms anyone for the better.

God's love upholds the universe, whether I believe it or not. God fully loves me warts and all, whether I believe it or not. My imperfections will not change that one bit. God unreservedly loves everyone and everything and has no heart to do otherwise. If only people could accept that. Even Christians may struggle with this idea. The message of being a sinner and that is why Jesus had to die that horrible death rings loudly still. Jesus died to redeem a massive creation that *exists* in him. That for a reason only God knows, became infiltrated with the power of sin from its very beginning. That I would have to carry blame for that is preposterous. I will have to owe up for my moral failings for sure and in this I am a sinner. But one forgiven in Christ by God's love and understanding.

How then will I get a feel for God's incredible love towards me? Simply, I will have to accept it to be true and not let negative thoughts stand in the way. There is much in my soul that could try to convince of my unworthiness. But it makes no sense before a loving God, who declares me worthy in Christ. God's love that IS, will bring me into the freedom of Jesus, the Lord. My faith has made me whole.

4
A Mundane God

The word mundane has an interesting history. During the 12th century it stood for 'pure, clean elegant; noble and generous.' Its Latin origin is the word *mundus* that means 'world'. The word was used when translating the word *kosmos* in the writings of an ancient Greek philosopher Pythagoras in reference to 'the universe as an embodiment of order and harmony.' Come the 15th century and *mundanus* meant 'belonging to the world' as distinct from the church. Then finally from about 1850 onward mundane became what it means today: 'dull and not interesting'.

There is lots in this short paragraph that reminds me of God and a few aspects that don't. The idea that the Lord would be boring and uninteresting is incorrect. Non-believers may think so but not to a committed Christian.

Then there is the use of the word mundane in separating 'the world' from 'the church'. That idea would have come about with the development of astronomy and physics as sources of truth in contrast to Scripture. This perception prevails in the modern mind that considers science and church to be incompatible. Many a Christian scientist though will not hold that view.

I like the word mundane with regard to God in the Pythagorean sense. The universe and the incredible dynamics that unify it are an astounding handiwork. Its 12th century use associated with pure, noble and generous also reminds of God. Even the modern meaning of mundane as 'nothing special' and bringing rather little excitement appeals to me. Many of God's everyday influences are not detected and hide within the mundane. It needs a special feel to sense that.

A friend of mine loves going bush to sit under the starry skies in solitude. Often he senses the Lord interacting with his spirit in special ways. But not so last time. 'That's okay,' he said. 'It was nice just sitting there with the Lord.' There is great wisdom in that comment. Perhaps the Lord decided for him to stand solely on his own two legs, those of the renewed spirit within him. The knowledge that he is divinely loved and that God is always near whatever the situation.

For healthy, Christian living it is essential to become familiar with the everyday, mundane God. We don't go to church to find God, but to worship and learn. Yes, the service may lift the spirit but it doesn't mean anything with regard to God's presence. The God of church is exactly the same as the God of daily life. Whether the spirit is uplifted or down, God is near. In the vagaries of everyday the divine is present. It is important to come to grips with God in the mundane for that is where my strength of spirit shines. In days when I hold it together expressing the nature of Jesus as best I can.

A song by *We Five* begins with the line, 'When I woke up this morning, you were on my mind.' It's a nice, upbeat piece of music. I have grown to wake up with Jesus on my mind before I ever step out of bed. It comes naturally and is a habit that can be learned simply by practising it. Just ask the Holy Spirit to remind you. It is a great start to the day. I then often say a 'hail Jesus' in my mind/spirit while going about my business. How does it feel, to have the Lord with me in the mundane? Somehow I just sense it and it is a mystery. A mystery available to anyone who seeks it wholeheartedly.

5

Good Enough

Recently, I was reading up on Epicurus, born on the Greek island of Samos in 341 BC. His philosophy focused on what it would mean to live a life of pleasure. Not in a hedonistic way, though Epicurus and his followers knew how to enjoy himself, but in a wise way. How to be satisfied with what was on offer and manage unhelpful desires. Being content rather than always aiming for that just-a-bit- more. Like: I just finished this chocolate bar if only I could have just a bit more. Our car is totally adequate, but wouldn't it be nice to have a new one. My situation in life is rather okay, it would be better though if…..!

Not that any of these desires are necessarily wrong, the problem is that they diminish the pleasure of life by highlighting what is perceived as lacking. When what is happening to me is not quite good enough rather than being grateful for what is. The book I am reading sums it up: 'Good enough represents an attitude of deep gratitude toward whatever happens to you.' I subscribe to that in spite of its difficulties. My wife and I have some plans for the future that cannot presently be activated but one day will come to pass. We talk about it in the understanding that really, our present situation is surely good enough. The Lord has his timing and we will wait while enjoying our current circumstances with pleasure and thanksgiving. (Since writing this the Lord has acted in a clear demonstration of providence.)

'Good enough' is a popular concept in parenting as well. Years ago, Dr Donald Winnicot observed the wellbeing of thousands of babies and in 1953 published the book, 'Good Enough Mother.' His insights are popular today in parental psychology. A key insight is that when infants and young children are positively responded to with care, and the parent 'fails' them in non-damaging ways, those children will develop a measure of independence. It will teach the child to tolerate frustration and waiting, which is a positive towards coping. Parents who do their best need not feel guilty when the inevitable moments of not being available, or not getting it quite right, occur. Good enough parenting is good enough.

Good enough is essential in having a feel for God. It prevents dissatisfactions marring that sense of contentment before the Lord. About difficulties Apostle Paul advises: 'In everything by prayer and supplication with thanksgiving let your requests be made known to God. And the peace of God, which passes all understanding, will keep your hearts and your minds in Christ Jesus' (Phil. 4:6-7). Thanksgiving applies both to the problem being solved in God's time and to gratefulness towards God regardless of circumstances.

When at times the Lord feels absent and unconcerned about my problems, the perfect Parent may possibly apply the principle of good enough. My waiting and frustration builds spiritual character, so invaluable in the challenges of life. My being familiar with good enough will then help me in maintaining that feel of the Lord's presence. When I will decide that my situation is sufficient and in accordance with what God has in store for me. Concluding that, 'Ah well, it's good enough Lord,' brings some rest to my soul. Not that when in dire straits I won't add, 'Please help!'

I think Epicurus is onto something. Be grateful for the small things each day. An indifferent cup of coffee can be enjoyed like a good one when being not too picky about it. After all, it's still coffee. The indifferent and the good to a large extent are mental states. Good enough does bring a lot of pleasure into life when in my mind it becomes 'good' and I am satisfied. What the Lord brings me each day I will aim to consider good enough. I will seek to enjoy his goodness. It feels good!

6

Love and Logic

Logic is the art of reasoning correctly. For such reason to be effective a framework is needed. Mathematics is such a framework and very powerful in getting results that stand up. Much of modern technology is derived from it. In every field of knowledge logic is operative at least to some extent. Basically, it is a matter of aligning cause and effect.

Frameworks of logic however differ greatly and determine insights. In philosophy, for instance, explaining reality as an idealist or materialist results in varied out-comes. The first takes mind and consciousness as its starting point whereby those qualities reach beyond the physical. The second holds that matter is the fundamental substance in nature, that the body that makes human awareness possible and contains it. Theology is idealist with the universe an expression of

God's ideas. In the interpretation of these different views logic invariably applies.

Mathematics is a 'neutral' framework of logic in that feelings are not integrate to its design. They may have a role in how a practitioner feels to progress in using mathematics but no further. Not so with philosophy and theology where a personal sense of what being alive is about will shape the approach to understanding. Libraries full have been written presenting suggestions and insights always using logic in support of making a case. So, when considering God, the ultimate being, what feel would be the starting point in gaining the best understanding?

God *is* Love and that I believe should override all that relates to the knowledge of divine reality. Whatever is perceived as from God must satisfy the test of love. In case love is not immediately apparent like in a suffering creation, revelation may point towards love yet being operative. If in an idea or representation of God love cannot be detected, then the proposition doesn't correctly represent the divine. Let me give an example.

A verse in the Lord's Prayer reads: 'But lead us not into temptation.' As if God would ever contemplate such a thing. Apostle James writes that God tempts no one, is incapable of it (1:13). Logically, in light of God's nature, the verse is wrong. Could Jesus ever have said such a thing? Perhaps the original would have read differently. In considering this verse a feel for what God is like, that love will never tempt, must be applied. The verse following, about delivering us from the evil one, helps in perceiving what Jesus is alluding to. Lord keep me from temptation and evil away from me, whereby the temptation would involve serious wrongdoing. Love being logically applied is central in interpreting Scripture. When confusion arises, which it often does, then love must weigh heaviest.

When love cannot be detected, God is not rightly represented. Anything that is good and brings wellbeing into life is a manifestation of love. This is the measure by which to determine whether something aligns with the expressions and purposes of God. This principle is much maligned, already was in the days of Jesus and before, and it continues today. Seeking for love is logical in matters of God and when found ensures a correct perspective.

It is what put Jesus at loggerheads with the religious authorities of his day. In the Gospels this struggle features prominently. When Jesus declared himself to be the Son of God, the Jews took up stones to kill him as a blasphemer. In his defence the Lord referred to the miracles he had been doing as the works of his Father.

Can't you see how incredible and good those are, he suggested. If in spite of that you cannot believe in me as the Christ at least believe that the works are because of the Father is in me and I am in the Father (John 10:36-38). It was to no avail.

Logic can be a slippery slope when based on facts that are wrong. The religious leaders could justify their unbelief because biblically the Christ was to come from Bethlehem, while Jesus was from Nazareth in Galilee. When facts become involved, the logic may be right but the outcomes can be faulty. Jesus suggested that works showing love and care should override facts. Facts may be right or wrong, but when God's love is on display they must never hinder a recognition of that love.

A true fact is that God *is* Love. It is the best starting point to Christian understanding. Love is not a singular fact but a powerful dynamic by which everything exists in Christ. Every person has the ability to express love and to evaluate what confronts accordingly. When love is lacking, when what is good is missing; whether in an action or in what is written, God is not expressed correctly. Applying this approach to Scripture will have its challenges, but necessary ones. The test of love is a simple logic. 'If I have not love, I am nothing,' Apostle

Paul said (1Cor. 13:2). Without being of charitable disposition, I will not have a feel for God, nor will I rightly understand the Lord. In light of the nature of God, that is logical.

7

Rhyme nor Reason

The saying that there is rhyme nor reason to a situation is well known. When neither poetic detection nor mental deduction will bring any sense to it. For instance, for someone familiar to act completely out of character is baffling. Why on earth did that happen? A question that is also pertinent when it applies to God, when instances recorded in Scripture seem to completely deny the divine nature. Such as God being seen as a God of war who instructs the Israelites to kill all the men and male children of the enemy plus every woman who is not is a virgin (Num. 31: 17) God's ways may be higher than ours, but this simply cannot resonate. There is rhyme nor reason to it. The logic of love tells me that God must have been misunderstood.

The understanding of God has been progressive. Only with the arrival of Jesus, his resurrection and the wisdom given by God to the first Apostles, became the revelation of who God really is complete. That God *is* Love, has a good plan, and is fully in control of our world and its future.

The knowledge of God as it evolved from Abraham onward has always been partial and culturally conditioned. The Bible is a book of history, about a people coming to grips with the One God. Much of it involves strife with the nations surrounding Israel and disagreements within their own community. God was their spiritual point of reference, a point that they could only comprehend in accordance with the culture of their day. The prophets who spoke on behalf of God often were mistreated. Scripture is as much a record of human affairs as it is a history of God's involvement in our world and being understood and misunderstood. The Bible must be read with this in mind.

Christian history is no different. The Inquisition, years ago, tortured people to help them change their 'heretic' beliefs so that they would end up in heaven instead of hell. Witch hunts were a fight against the Devil while, in fact, by their nature should be understood as from the Devil. All off this because of Church teaching. Early scientists were burned at the stake because their

Rhyme nor Reason 27

ideas didn't line up with biblical understanding as dictated by the Church. Insights into the nature of God and Scripture were subject to interpretations guided by human preferences and culture. Little has changed today. Admittedly, the Bible can be a difficult book to understand and allows for finding justifications of behaviours that may seem biblically justified but do not measure up to the standards of what love is about. Whether affairs of Church or world, the Lord seems content with working in the background in accordance with the divine wisdom. Whereby those who reach out and come in close will be able to find him and truly know him.

Our world is subject to the massively destructive influences of the power of sin. It brings significant trouble into a person's life with many a struggle. Things may be demanded that to a caring person simply are inhuman. Like going into combat and killing, which a friend of mine was forced into via a ballot by government decree. The Lord told him that he would not be held responsible for his involvement in the war defending himself. God understands that a fallen creation makes terrible things happen. That there seems no end to it and the why is a matter I have no answer to. I'm convinced that one day God will make all things well – in heaven. On earth nobody will be held responsible for the dynamics of sin within creation as such. At a personal level the deficiencies and mistakes to owe up to before the Lord are the serious ones, surely wilful immoral choices that classify as evil. Then heartfelt repentance becomes necessary.

The mystery of God often remains just that. When rhyme nor reason confronts me, I let it be. Much involving the Lord must be taken at faith value, when what is facing me is confusing. Faith value brings the right perspective to life and rest in the conviction that God is good. Whatever my circumstances, I do best in resigning myself in the knowledge that the Lord knows best and will work things out for the humility of faith. There may be little rhyme to it and my intuitive sensing of what really is happening comes up short. Reasoning it out will not help much either. There is only one logic that feels right and measures up in such circumstances: that God *is* Love and can be trusted, always.

8

Invitation or Submission

When an invitation to a party arrives in the mail a decision must be made of whether I will accept or not. It is up to me. When a summons from the court comes my way I have little option but to attend. Not doing so has unpleasant consequences. Unlike with the party, my freedom to decline has been taken away. I will have to submit.

The parable of the great banquet (Luke: 15-24) tells of the Lord organising an incredible party. But those who should well know how fine a function it will be all make rather lame excuses and decide not to come. Servants of the Lord are sent into the highways and byways calling out the invitation. They are told to be compelling as best they can. 'You *must* come, it will be sooo good!' Though the Lord would be capable of forcing people to attend that never happened. The invitation to the great banquet did not impede on the will of those invited. They were free to make up their minds.

God is love and never will do submission. Reading Scripture in places, it may seem that submission is required. Like the Ten Commandments each starting with the imposing phrase of, 'Thou shalt not!' How though might it be best understood? When a parent and child cross the road and a car comes their way, that parent will instruct the child to stop and possibly take hold of the young one. 'Don't!' will be the message. When an adult crosses the road that 'don't' will not involve a restraint. The adult is well aware of what is best in the situation. 'Thou shalt not', must be read in that way. It is God's strong advice towards avoiding calamity. The wisdom of it became clear when Israel decided to ignore God's instructions with dire consequences. The Ten Commandments are given as a way towards a happy and homogeneous society. They are positive and not over-bearing. The choice is ours.

The Lord invites, always, and never will subdue the will of a person. Offering free will is what love is about. It puts the ball in the people's court, which can become a stumbling block. It surely was one to those invited to the banquet. Jesus was highlighting the many blind spots of believers who are smug in knowing God. When religious tradition and ritual offers a framework of being spiritual that can make comfortable. When human control over the worship of God erases the sensitivity of what God's Spirit really is about. When love is brought under submission within the human heart to the point of an illusionary spirituality. When the right feel for God has become impossible.

The parable of the banquet was given in response to a self-assured comment about the Kingdom of God by a diner who sat with Jesus at table. Don't fool yourself, the Lord explained. You may think to have it sorted, but better be careful not to miss the boat. I must watch out against spiritual self-satisfaction and the only true antidote to that is humility. I am invited to enjoy the treasures of the Kingdom and must be careful not to become mesmerised with the fool's gold that is available in religious tradition. The Lord will warn against it in my spirit, which I am free to ignore. God's love will guide, but is never forceful. As mentioned, God does not do submission.

The freedom of will allowed by God is a divine wisdom. The very nature of love is to bring liberation. It is both a blessing and a difficulty. It is easy for people to go astray being overtaken by desires and ego-centricity. The Lord may not do submission, but the church surely can. Also, the church can be a place of love and often is. The challenge is to detect what is happening. A feel for God will make it clear. It helps my discernment and tells me to be a person of love, to never be self-satisfied and overbearing.

9

Enthused or Excited

Titillation and excitement are the order of the day in the modern media. The words amazing, incredible and extreme are what headlines are made of. Every news item scrambles for attention and much of popular reporting is over the top. Objectivity goes by the wayside for it will not attract an audience and the advertising dollars associated with it. We are living with hyped up news cycles giving brief information that is often not of great significance and lasts for a limited time before the next minor event presented as major and exciting comes along.

God is no stranger to getting the attention when it really matters. The miracles Jesus did served that purpose. Understandably, people flocked to find out what this man was like. Thousands followed the Lord into open spaces away from the towns. A number of times miraculously he fed them multiplying a few loaves and fishes. They ate their fill with baskets of food left over. Our God offers divine abundance.

A group of people kept following Jesus to which he responded that they did so because of being well fed physically. But they paid far less attention to what his miracles *really* were about: the presence of his Father in heaven who sought to help them renew their lives. I am the real bread you need, Jesus told them, the living bread. If you eat of that bread, you will live forever. 'And the bread I will give for the life of the world is my flesh.' With the spiritual eyes of their hearts blinded, they decided that the Lord must be deranged and walked away (John 6).

Everyone likes a bit of excitement at times. It stimulates the soul and makes one feel good. Certain styles of church worship make good use of this need for stirred up feelings. God is awesome and amazing and on our side. That is true enough. But when worship reaches no further spiritually than the eating of loaves and fishes, the being energised in God will be superficial. Eating the living bread is quite different.

In the past I have been involved with charismatic conferences at a leadership level and much good was achieved in those events. They were uplifting times. I have attended services to which many were drawn because of someone with a healing ministry. Miracles do happen. I have also heard of believers flying internationally to be part of the latest excitement seemingly on the Lord's calendar for then to share about it importantly once back home. I began to wonder. At one place, far away from Australia, God apparently split a pulpit in half. During a lecture at my college it came up and I told the student: 'So what? What's the big deal? If the creator of the universe cannot split a pulpit such a God is not worthy of believing in. God is just as present here now, as with that miraculous event. I don't need miracles to believe in the Lord. And surely I won't chase after them.'

Not that God's miracles aren't wonderful. The Lord has done many of those in history and it will continue. But seeking the excitement of God is not what true believing in about. Instead of being excited there is a far better word whereby to measure the dynamics within my soul. It is the reality of being 'enthused'. The roots of this word in Greek are a combination of *en* (in) and *theos* (god) indicating divine inspiration. Enthusiasm is far better at eliciting a feel for God than excitement will ever be. Being enthused has an energising calmness about it that reflects the divine rest. No froth and bubbles. A calm that dwells deeply within and nourishes the spirit with the bread of new life.

There is an excitement about with the notion that soon the Lord will come back. A great deal of energy is spent on this topic. Admittedly, the Return is coming closer every day, as it has been throughout Christian history. Many times Christ's return has been considered as imminent. I often say to the Lord please do come back for the world is in such a mess with great suffering. It is a calm prayer totally without excitement. Making sure of having oil in my lamp is my prime concern. Excitability is like a fog in a breeze. Being enthused in the Lord carries the inspiration of the Holy Spirit. It is what keeps the flame burning.

10

Child or Champion

The world needs champions; people to admire. Their names are written into the annals of history, entered on honour rolls and, when really great, immortalised in statues. In modern days there are more champions than ever in a large variety of specialisations. Celebrity rules and coming first is the pinnacle. Lesser mortals, however talented and working hard, are destined to be also-rans. In team sports a fantastic player may be the best around but if his team never wins a trophy his or her legacy will be tainted. It makes little sense, but that is how society functions.

Who is the greatest, is an age-old question that troubled the disciples in Jesus' days. They were wondering who amongst them would be tops. The Lord called a child unto himself and said, 'When you receive a child, you are receiving me.' What Jesus was alluding to is that important people tend to take little notice of the non-important. High ambitions can limit one's view of what really matters – the significance of everyone: young and old, rich or poor.

At one instant parents were trying to bring children to the Lord but were obstructed by the disciples. Jesus became indignant, rebuked his companions, and said: 'Let the children come to me, do not hinder them; for to such belongs the kingdom of God. Truly, I say to you, whoever does not receive the kingdom of God like a child shall not enter it.' Jesus took the children in his arms and blessed them, laying his hands upon them (Mark 10: 13-16).

Talents are to be made the best of, but the value of being good at something must be kept in perspective. The idea of being a great person would never have crossed the Lord's mind. It just is not what a feel for God is about. The ways of God are different from the skewed manner in which much of the world goes about its business. God's ways are higher, not only because of the divine wisdom and ability, but also when expressed in personhood. Jesus spoke a lot about the kingdom of God which his listeners those days would have understood as a rulership on earth. Not so, Jesus explained, the kingdom of God is within you, referring to a new way of living inspired by the Holy Spirit (Luke 17:21). Its dynamics are one of dependency on the Lord not unlike a child with a parent.

No longer a child I reached the age of accountability long ago. The world and its egocentricity, its need for identifying with heroes and champions, confronts me like it does everyone. The cult of celebrity adoration is reaching silly proportions. The temptations of being important infiltrate all facets of society including the Church. Unless you become like a child, Jesus forewarned, you will miss what I am about. It is then not my kingdom that is expressed from within you, but the old ways of unregenerate being. Your religion will not save you from this reality.

The word that always comes to mind in finding God's ways is humility. It is the humble who notice the children and those down on their luck. My growing up from a child into adulthood has hardened me and has robbed me of a precious freedom. In my book *Drawings and Reflections*, with the drawings by my wife Jeanne, there is a little story.

***

Sunny-side Up

With sunny-side up the yoke remains runny. Once-over and the egg becomes firm. A good childhood is like that. Over time, it becomes flipped and my soul solidifies. In our world I need a mind of my own. I become rather inflexible.

But must the sunny-side of childhood be lost altogether? Apostle Paul suggests a renewing of my mind. Mostly that is understood as holiness thinking. But there is more to it. The renewal includes a liberation from defensive thought processes in which I am pitted against society. I must become less hardened – soften up.

Jesus desires to set me free from cynicism into tolerance. From seeing the world as a mess into knowing God to be mysteriously at work towards a great ending. That kind of thinking brings the sunny-side back into my soul.

***

A feel for God includes the regaining of childlike simplicity, flexibility and trust. I must be soft and sensitive at heart. The kingdom of God is not a rulership, but a relational dynamic in accordance with the nature of Christ. Competition is not what I should be about, but doing my best is. Popularity is a pitfall.

11

Faith and Fragmentation

The history of the Jewish and Christian faith is very much one in which preferred beliefs will invariably find support from scriptural interpretation. It can then be argued and even fought over. It may seem that God purposefully confuses the faithful so that divine realities become difficult to understand. The problem, of course, is not due to God, but because of human susceptibility to the vagaries of sin that clouds good judgement and encourages some to become masters over many others in what to believe. For worshipers of the One God that would involve the rulership of religious authorities. Differences in ideas often set one believer against the other. The nature of the One God, who is Love, thus is violated and the Holy Book's main intent is misunderstood. The idea of God is held hostage to how culture is conditioned by those in command.

With the Enlightenment what is written in the Bible came under the scrutiny of ever evolving scholarship. Theology and philosophy began to address the meaning and contradictions of the Bible linguistically and historically relying on the proficiency of a reasoned approach. The inerrancy of scripture became challenged and with good reason. It is true that interpretations that disregard the supernatural, like the existence of miracles, overstepped the mark and were thus noted. But the notion, mentioned before, that the Bible is a history of people who learned to understand their God over a long period of time, with many a misinterpretation, is correct. Events are recorded as having happened by divine guidance that are gruesome. Such as Gideon having his followers kill 42.000 Ephraimites because they could not say the word 'shibboleth' accurately (Judges 12:6). The progressive revelation of divine intentions is underscored by the Jewish belief not including a clearly stated afterlife. That reality finally was introduced by Jesus Christ.

Philosopher Immanuel Kant held that God has placed reason and morality within human ability to guide good understanding – including that of Scripture. Ritchie Robertson in his book *The Enlightenment* (p. 119) quotes Kant. 'Allowing a supposedly divine voice or a divine book a higher authority than one's own moral intuitions would be contrary to reason and to human dignity.' Kant is especially known for pointing out that pure reason cannot explain all and is influenced by knowledge that is innate to personhood and independent of the intellect, such as knowing the good from evil.

I appreciate scholarship. It has helped me in coming to my own conclusions knowledgably. But in understanding the divine it has its limits. Too much fragmentation into categories and sub-categories robs an idea of its soul. The present enchantment with spirituality is a case in point. The more it is reasoned about the further it drifts away from the actual experience that spirituality alludes to. Much of the mystery of God will never be pierced by mere intellectual pursuit. Rather, the Lord has made sure that anyone with a heart so inclined can well understand him without much study at all. Though a basic idea of the Gospel is essential.

An accurate knowledge of God begins with the experience called faith. The sense that God exists; a conviction of things not seen which, with regard to God, are many. That, Jesus is the Son of God, who overpowered the sin that is ingrained in creation and rose again; who now offers a new life in the power of the Holy Spirit. All that must be taken by faith and then can be experienced as a sure knowing. Anything that reflects love, is positive and aligns with the nature of Christ, is of God. Anything that is incredible, but fits the narrative of who God is and the divine plan for creation, can be safely accepted as true in faith. Such as the universe having been created in Christ and holding together in him. These realities stand alone and any fragmentation in accordance with reason must be considered as of secondary importance and may do true understanding a disservice.

Keep it simple and don't overcomplicate things. All the questions you may wish to raise have already been debated in the history of Christianity and look where it got us. Disagreements and even hostility caused by varied interpretations of Scripture abound. Respect others in their opinions and avoid strife. Read your Bible with a feel for God and a freedom of making up your own mind about how to understand it. Your take on the written Word is of far less concern to the Lord than how you approach him, the living Word. Apostle John writes that there is no need that anyone would teach you for you have a special anointing of the Lord to trust in as your teacher (1John 2:27). Safeguard your insights with humility and openness to change. The way to God is by faith.

12

Rest or Restive

A central theme in Orthodox spirituality is the pursuit of *hesychasm*, which means 'coming to rest.' There is a well-known story of a pilgrim who in seeking to achieve this spiritual state was taught the Jesus Prayer. 'Lord Jesus, Son of God, have mercy on me a sinner.' After many days of mentally repeating the prayer it began to live in the heart of the pilgrim spontaneously. He had found his rest in God.

Coming to rest, that inner sense of wholesome togetherness, has always been a challenge. Personhood, by its very nature of being multi-facetted in many ways, will not find its rest easily. Many people rather would not come to rest for it might confront them with movements within their soul that are disturbing and best ignored. Others, when finding themselves in moments of in-activity, immediately decide that they are bored – a problem to be solved. Society at large is not geared towards rest but towards interaction. An energetic bustle rules the day.

It is particularly so in cities and a main reason for their attraction. Cities have a restive air giving the impression that something is fermenting unseen. An energy that many find attractive. It is absorbed within the psyche and conditions it. A sense of restiveness, that mild agitation deep within, lingers in everyone though, irrespective of where they are. That feeling of being unsettled for some reason. It is what the pilgrim sought to still.

Being restive is a deeper emotion than restlessness. It is difficult to put your finger on what exactly is bothering and the best response is to simply get on with life. The feeling of being restless is different. Usually its reason is understood and a wilful response is possible. I have regularly felt restless, particularly in spring with the weather improving. The dynamics at play within my soul were clear.

Not so with being restive, a feeling that sometimes rose up disturbingly within me, particularly when the Lord began to twig my inner being towards greater psycho-spiritual health. At one time I felt that a soul adjustment was on the cards. I was not happy with myself and said, 'I must change, Lord help me!' This agitation went on for some days, not that anyone was to notice. I knew change was coming. One morning I woke up at peace again and felt different, much to my delight. It was subtle, but something good had happened. The Lord had decided the time for me to mature a little further had arrived. The feeling of rest I usually enjoy had returned.

Not that my inner rest is not regularly disturbed. There are all kinds of dissatisfactions and challenges niggling within me, just what ordinary living is about. Those are for me to deal with, not the Lord, but with the help of his spirit. The difficulties may be annoying but do not diminish my deeper peace. A solid time of prayerful reflection and my troubles are put into perspective.

The pilgrim sought rest for his soul and undertook a long journey searching everywhere in finding it. Jesus knew all about the problem and had advice, a simple invitation. 'Come to me, and I will give you rest,' he said. Learn from me. I will not make it difficult for you. I know it is not easy to find rest for your soul and I will be gentle (Matt. 11:28-30).

Thing is: am I sufficiently aware of this need for rest within my soul and the help on offer by the Lord? Or am

I just doggedly living on being a good Christian paying the naturally restive nature of my psyche little attention. The journey towards inner peace never happens automatically. I must set upon it, stick with it, and notice my feel for the Lord deepen. Only the Lord offers a rest that is of God. The journey never ends and brings many a still water.

13

Conscience and Compassion

An awareness guided by conscience is exclusively a human ability. In the animal world it is not found. The word conscience comes from the Latin *conscientia* meaning to live with an inherent knowledge that the Bible recognises as discerning good from evil, what is right from wrong. This notion opens up to a wide array of possibilities as to what is okay and what is not. The question is relevant to all of life. Throughout the ages every branch of human knowledge – from the religious, philosophical and societal –has written extensively on the topic.

The word 'conscience' is not found in Scripture but is situationally alluded to: like when Jesus was confronted with a woman found in adultery and suggested that those without sin throw the first stone (John 8: 3-11). While the parable of the Good Samaritan presents a traveller moved in his consciences towards a generous act of compassion (Luke 10: 29-37). Conscience is an innate ability that is culturally conditioned also. What is right or wrong in life and how to best respond can present real difficulties. 'Here I stand, I can do no else,' said Martin Luther facing a Roman Catholic inquisition. A strong feeling convinced him that his actions were justifiable and necessary.

Conscience is a deep and varied experience with many dynamics in play. It has been compared to an 'inner light', which is an apt description for Christian understanding. But this light may not shine brightly, or at all. A compassionate conscience brings most benefit towards psycho-spiritual health. A conscience that is judgemental declares guilt, while an indifferent one simply does not care. Psychopaths are so known because they lack any sense of a conscience.

God has placed conscience within human awareness so that people may have a sense of what God is like. Conscience unveils the divine nature and by being exposed to the negative as the opposite of the good, it accentuates that nature. I would have no idea what God is like, unless I have an idea what God is not like. Sin is sin because it is not God. My conscience is my guiding light on life's journey and originates with God. Within my spirit a dynamic is operative that inspires me to make the journey a good one.

Conscience is fundamental in being human. It reflects God within personhood and rates highly in interacting with the Lord. Life is evaluated by the standards of good and evil. When Jesus offers rest for the soul it surely includes a conscience that is at ease. A feel for God is of importance in this. A sense of the goodness of God is essential in my arriving at a conscience sufficiently pacified for it to be of little bother. A feel that tells me all is okay between the Lord and me, for I have put my good and bad cards on the table. The latter need redeeming and wiped clean.

To have a conscience all stilled takes time. As I have walked with Jesus over the years the constraints of conscience have guided and taught me. Always seeking the good of the other has limited the need of those constraints and these days I have little need of them. Compassion, or charity if a less emotionally laden word is preferred, is the balm that sanctifies conscience. A conscience at rest is a great blessing and possible with the Lord.

Of course, I have failed at times and made mistakes that troubled my conscience. But rather than becoming judgmental towards myself and feeling ever guilty, I have embraced my frailties before the Lord. I have asked for forgiveness and been compassionate towards my own person. The Lord has wiped my guilt away and I have accepted it. Guilt must not linger once the Lord has wiped the slate clean. It is one of the great miracles towards a renewal of the soul. It is good to ask the Lord for a clear feeling of this to be true; a feeling he would give anyway, which I must not hinder by a doubt that may rise preventing it. Not that the memories of my failings don't still sting at times, but such is life. It keeps me alert not to fall for the same mistakes again.

Conscience is indeed an inner light. Its brightness will be spoiled to an extent for such is the human condition. The Lord came to sharpen my inner light with a redemptive power that outshines everything.

14

Angry or Aggrieved

Anger is a destructive emotion that affects wellbeing. It happens when feeling wrongly done by. A lingering resentment takes joy out of the soul and unfortunately is what many people are facing. Being angry is the most common human of conditions. In an imperfect world reasons for it will inevitably arrive. It can be so caustic an experience that Jesus gave that most cryptic advice of turning the other cheek. Only forgiveness will ever undo the potential damage deep seated anger can cause. Apostle Paul urged to deal with it swiftly and not to let the sun go down on anger. All good suggestions, if only it were that easy. Anger will always be a struggle. On occasion inevitably I will be angry or will be exposed to it.

Besides anger affecting me directly, it may arrive because of what I see is done to others. A righteous anger can be an honourable condition. Like when the Lord cleansed the Temple with a whip being stirred about how a holy place of worship dedicated to his heavenly Father had become a den of money changers and thieves. But surely, as soon as the act was done, all his agitation would have vanished. Anger, whether righteous or not, must be nipped in the bud. Being angry becomes an emotional infection when it keeps on smouldering. Then, I must discuss it with the Lord and ask for help.

But, you might say, God can be angry. There are quite a few examples of that in the Bible. The thought that it is a terrible thing to fall into the hand of an angry God has been used effectively by the Church as a reason for salvation and to keep believers subservient (Hebr. 10: 31). However, how can a God who *is* Love and perfectly at rest in Spirit succumb to an emotion as negative as anger that originates from the dynamics of sin? After all, in heaven there will be no sin and thus no anger. I suggest that using the word anger with regard to God would have been culturally relevant but is factually incorrect. Love and anger don't mix.

There are other words, milder than anger, to be used in expressing how God might feel about a situation. For instance, God could be aggrieved or indignant. God may be displeased or annoyed. None of these words carry the destructive quality of anger. Presenting God as a just and an angry punisher has done great harm to how the divine nature is perceived. The way in which God will be just, is for God to decide. How humans under the influences of sin might wrongly project their ideas about justice onto the divine wisdom is immaterial. Justice belongs to the Lord.

With the gods generally being a projection of human experience dressed up in a transcendental cloak, they would be able of anger and must be appeased. This idea of what gods are like was assigned also unto the One God of Abraham. The arrival of Jesus did not undo the notion of an angry God, however much the Lord presented his Father as loving and good. Apostle Paul, the first Christian theologian, wrote most eloquently about the importance of love. His mystical experiences must have impressed this upon him. And yet, the writer of Hebrews (I don't consider Paul the author) used the Old Testament to state anew that God had declared, 'Vengeance is mine, I will repay' (Hebr. 10:30). It doesn't make sense to ascribe this intention a God who *is* Love.

The statement that God is love had to wait till the Gospel of John had been written well after Hebrews. The idea of what God was really like developed over time – a very long one. Lady Julian of Norwich, during the Middle Ages, wrote the most elaborate and insightful explanation of the Lord's love based on her visions. And it was only in our days that those became well-known and popular. One of her insights was that there is no anger to be found in God, only inexhaustible love. God has the final word with regard to creation, she saw, and one day will make all things well.

I worship a God of love and not of anger. A God who is just, but in a divine way that is beyond human understanding. Anger is a human emotion, negative and destructive. I am careful to succumb to it as little as possible and will seek to turn my anger into being indignant and aggrieved. That feels right before the Lord. That feels like what God is about.

15

Agapino

A story I wrote based on the Revelations of Julian of
Norwich for my book *Julian's Windows*
(References are in brackets)

Agapino, a beautiful little angel, appeared before God in heaven and was received with much delight. 'You're looking tired, Agapino,' the Lord observed.

'It's hard work spreading love about on earth, Lord,' the little angel confessed.

'You tell me about it,' the Lord agreed.

'I have to fight all that suffering and pain. It's difficult to pierce through it and make love relevant.'

'Yes, but you know the pain, it has to be, I'm afraid.' It was not the first time that God had told the little angel this. 'Just wait till you see for yourself where it is leading. I will explain that to everyone one day.' (1)

'I know you will do a great deed Lord, far greater than anyone can ever imagine. It will make all things well.' (2)

Agapino had no problem with that. Whatever the Lord said, it would be so.

'Oh yes!' God confirmed. 'Do you remember my servant Job, whom you tried to encourage? He was blessed doubly after all his suffering.'

'It was not of much help to him while he sat in ashes,' Agapino observed carefully.

'No, not then,' God had to admit. 'It hurt him, and me a lot, but it had to be.'

There was a moment of reflective silence in heaven.

'Some people I cannot get through to,' Agapino reported. 'They know not love,'

'Some are of the devil's condition,' God explained. 'Don't waste your time there. I won't have them mentioned in my sight, for now.' (3)

Agapino let that be.

'Most of them I find just have been blinded,' the little angel concluded. 'What they are really looking for I can offer, but they ignore me.' (4)

'You will have to suffer that Agapino, and keep working on a breakthrough,' God insisted. 'All the blind I keep alive within my heart. I hold them dear.' (5)

'Even though, they are fallen?' Agapino questioned.

'I don't blame them for that. (6) That is our problem – Mine, my Servant Son (7) and our Spirit. It has been solved.'

'They all have fallen, Lord,'

'They all live in my heart – apart from those of the devil, who are but a few.'

'How about those who have Jesus as their Saviour,' Agapino asked knowing the answer. The angel just took delight in hearing it.

'You know full well Agapino,' God answered with pleasure. 'Those are special. Not only are they in my heart, I dwell within theirs in a wonderful way.' (8)

'But even Christians can be hopeless with love, Lord,' the little angel complained.

'Come on, Agapino, straighten your back.' God smiled warmly. 'You must always take pleasure from those who understand salvation. I do.'

'Some understand it well,' Agapino had to admit. 'They can see love even when in pain.'

'They are my treasure,' God said. 'They know that I'm hurting with them. They will just have to trust that I will make all things very well one day.'

'Others don't live in accordance to what they confess though,' Agapino ventured.

'They should know better.'

'But you are not angry about that?

'Angry? (9) Have you ever seen anger in me, Agapino?

The little angel shook the head.

'My wrath is simply displeasure and a display of holiness, but it is not anger.' God was adamant on that. 'My wrath is because I love them and they behave stupidly.'

'So, you are also not angry with those who don't know you?'

'How can I be angry, if anger is not me, nothing like who I AM, Agapino?'

'So, you have a place for them somewhere?'

'I have a place for almost everybody. The first fruits, those who truly serve me while living on the earth, they will have their special rewards.' (10)

The little angel looked at God. Perhaps too many questions were being asked. However, God had divine patience.

'When people are hurting, they don't like me,' Agapino tried once again, for sympathy's sake.

'Often, they don't like me either, and I AM God,' was the answer.

'So, what do I tell everyone?' the angel of love persisted.

'What I've told you many times, Agapino.' God looked at the little servant kindly.

'That you love them more than they can ever know, and that counts almost everybody in.'

God nodded.

'That you understand their suffering and suffer likewise. (11) They just have to try accepting that.'

God nodded.

'That you look after those who have died.'

God nodded.

'And that you take great pleasure in those who are reaching out for you during their earthly lives. You are willing to be a friend to them.' (12)

God nodded. 'I'm closer than their breathing.' (13)

'That's good news, Lord,' Agapino said.

'You've got it, my little friend. You've got it.' God smiled. 'Go with speed on your way and keep the chin up.'

Referenced from *Julian of Norwich – Showings* 1978, Paulist Press, New York, (The Long Text)

1 Chapters 27 – p. 226; 85 – p. 341
2 Chapter   32 – p. 232
3 Chapter   33 – p. 234
4 Chapters 51 – p. 272; 52 – p. 280
5 Chapter   79 – p. 334
6 Chapters 27 – p. 226; 50 – p. 266
7 Chapters 51 –52
8 Chapter   72 – p. 320
9 Chapters 46 – p. 259; 49 – p.p. 263, 264
10 Chapters 39 – p. 245; 58 – p. 294
11 Chapter 28 – p. 227
12 Chapter 77 – p. 331
13 Chapter 72 – p. 72

AgapeDeum

Other books by Michael J Spyker

Being with God
Written in response to a disturbing vision. 'Let me help you in a troubled world,' the Lord says. How to find strength and benefits from being intimate with Jesus. *(Also free e-book)*

Walking with God
What are the essential pieces of the puzzle called 'God' and how will a concise explanation of their importance read? What will the full picture look like? *(Also free e-book)*

Meeting Emma
An introduction to Christian Spirituality in which Emma learns from theologian Joe how to involve God's spirit in everyday living.

Drawings and Reflections
52 short reflections on Christian vibrancy with full-colour illustrations by Jeanne Spyker Hardy.

Julian's Windows
A contemporary love story that contextualises many teachings of medieval mystic Lady Julian of Norwich.

The Language of Love
A love story that encourages wisdom and wellbeing, and seeking an authentic relationship with Jesus Christ.

Science and Spirit
How science and spirit exist is relation and what that means to Christian understanding.

The Primacy of Love
How a theological understanding that creation is essentially an expression of God's love leads to a model that explains the dynamics of human relating based on the Trinity.

Oh My Soul!
The meaning of soul, the roots of its awareness, and how soul health is helped by a Christian understanding of the dynamics involved.

Living Well
The art of making the best of life relationally. Though based on Christian insights this little book is meant for everyone and avoids religious references.

I Am Willing
A story about miracles and more based on the ministry of Dean Knight, who authors this little book with the help of Michael Spyker.

Shalomat
An adventure in which two young people are being chased across Australia while seeking to fulfil a riddle that has global consequences. The story is based on ideas from spirituality and philosophy.

Available at agapedeum.com

www.ingramcontent.com/pod-product-compliance
Lightning Source LLC
Chambersburg PA
CBHW072020290426
44109CB00018B/2296